Simple straightforward formula m

Casinos will not like this

Introduction

My name is Craig allin and what I will show you will change the way you stake forever , fingers crossed and good luck

This formula used in a responsible way will give you the upper edge in making a profit on a live casino or in a casino .
IT WILL NOT WORK ON A ROULETTE MACHINE AS A ROULETTE MACHINE AS ALL READY DECIDED THE OUTCOME BEFORE YOU EVEN SPIN .
Too many people you see playing these computers I like to call them convince themselves there is a method but there is not.
The computer as already decided if you are a winner or a loser !
I will show you in simple steps how you can place your chips to give you the upper hand most of the time but I will add it does require a substantial amount of funds in some cases to guarantee that return .
But everybody knows there is no 100% guarantee in anything ,
But I will show you and you will get it straight away without trailing through your average books which demand reading 500 pages .

The obvious

On this roulette wheel you see ....

18 reds numbers

18 black numbers

18 evens

18 odds

Which in insight will give you roughly 50% minus the green chance of winning if you were to back any of these with a 2/1 return .

Read on and you will see were im going with this .....

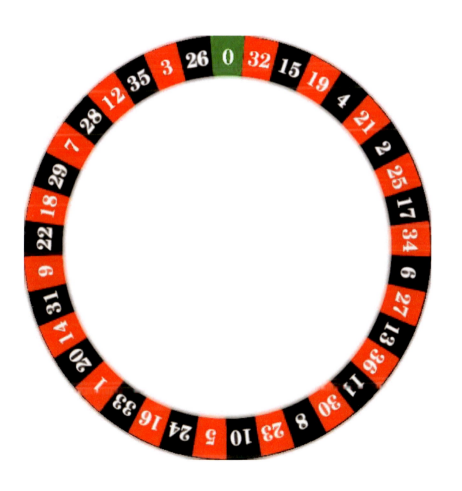

If I place £1 on even .
the outcome is odd .

The next spin ...
I place £3 on even .
the outcome is odd .

The next spin .....
I place £6 on even .
the outcome is odd .

The next spin ....
I place £12 on even .
the outcome is odd .

The next spin .....
I place £30 on even
the outcome is odd.

The next spin .....
I place £ 60 on even .
the outcome is odd .

The next spin ....
I place £130 on even .
the outcome is odd.

the next spin ....
I place £300 on even .
the outcome is odd .

the next spin ...
I place £ 650 on even
the outcome is odd .

The next spin ....
I place £1300 on even .
the outcome is odd .

The next spin ....
I place £3000 on even .
the outcome is odd .

The next spin ....
I place £7000 on even .
the outcome is EVEN !!!!!

Even after 12 spins that would still leave you with a
profit of £1,508.00

based on a 2/1 ratio .

As you can see the spins can go on and on without a win but eventually it would fall in your favour but the longer you go with out a spin that wins the higher the next stake would need to be , As you need to be able to cover your previous stakes during bets and enough to give you a profit on each spin when you get that win .

I know what your thinking ...

It can go on for 20 spins without a win .

But what you need to remember is eventually it will come in for you just like flipping a coin ten times .

the chances of it always landing on heads every time is very slim but yes it could happen .

Top tip for this formula

As shown on the previous page the worst case scenario it could take 12 spins or even more to get the result with profit .

Is there anyway of minimising the risk you may ask ?

The ancer is yes as on a online casino it will show you the previous spin results .

If you come across a table were the last 6 spins have been odds .

That would be the perfect table to start this formula you would say on evens ?

Or if the last 8 spins it as been red would that not be a obvious choice to back the formula on black ?

It takes a good eye for detail with what each table is doing and a lot of patience .

But if you sit back and really think on then you will see how easy it can be too make money at the table or online .

The profit

The key too profiting with this way of betting in my opinion is too walk away from that table or online game as soon as you win and move on to the next by looking out for that spin history to give you that upper hand once again .

Remember little profit is better then no profit .

Why not stop on that table or online game ?

Each player is different but is that not what the average player does by keep doubling each stake to get that big win and after a few spins you go all in on red leaving you with no balance .

Thats what the casinos want you to do .

Give you the small wins to entice you to bet bigger and empty everything you have .

Small wins then walk away .

Keep changing the tables looking out for the previous spin play to give you that upper hand .

Its the same with high numbers and low numbers .

the obvious if that last 8 numbers have been 1-18 .

The likelihood is in the next few spins it will be a high number and if you start that sequence and get the result you want on the sixth spin ,

Then you are still in profit of £8.

Wow £8 what a win you may say when ive staked £112 to get that little amount of profit ???

But what im trying to show you is the fundamentals of this betting pattern .

If you study the results then you will always walk a way a winner but its ultimately down to each player .

You may want to place your first spin with £5 on red and the outcome is black .

so for the second spin you want to place £25 on red to get that bigger profit .

It all works the same and gives you that upper hand if your studying the previous spin history .

Its all about knowing when to join that game play .

what you would ask yourself is ...

would you want to back red on a new table if that previous 4 spins have been red ?

Maybe or maybe not .

Example of a session on live casino roulette

Login to betting site ...
numerous amount of tables to choose from .
I will look into the spin history .....
First table I come across as a history of the last 3 spins being even numbers ....
So its a good place to start .

SESSION 1

ill put £1 on odd .
The outcome is even.

ill pertcefere and place £3 on on odd to cover my last stake and room for profit on this spin .
The outcome is odd .
I win £6 .
Which gives me a profit of £2 overall on this session .
ill leave this table session ......
(session time 2 minutes)

I look at the tables and come across a session were the last 5 spins have been low numbers so I join .

SESSION 2

I fancie £5 on a high number for the next spin
I place £5 on a high number .
The outcome is a high number .
I win £10 .

Which gives me a profit of £5 on this session .
I will leave the table session ....
(approx time 1 minute)

I look at the tables and come across a session were the
last 8 spins have been red numbers so I join .

SESSION 3

Ill put £1 on black .
The outcome is red .

Next spin ill place £3 on black .
The outcome is red .

Next spin ill place £6 on black .
the outcome is red.

Next spin ill place £15 on black .
The outcome is green zero

The next spin ill place £40 on black .
the outcome is black .
I win £80 .
Which gives me a profit of £15 .
ill leave this table session .....
(session time approximately 6 minutes)

I look at the tables and come across a table were the last 12 spins consist of high numbers so i join .

SESSION 4

Ill stake £1 on low numbers .
the outcome is high number .

The next spin I stake £5 on low numbers.
The outcome is high number .

The next spin I stake £15 on low numbers.
The outcome is low number .
I win £30 .
Which gives me a profit of £9 .
Ill leave the table session .....
(approximately table session time 5 minutes)

I look at the tables and come a table were the last 2 spins have been odd so I join.

SESSION 5

Ill stake £1 on even .
The outcome is even .
I win £2
Which gives me a profit of £1
Ill leave the table session .....
(approximately table session time 1 minute)

I look at the tables and a previous table I visited as a build of 5 spins on even so I join .

SESSION 6

Ill stake £1 on odd .
The outcome is even.

The next spin I stake £3 on odd .
The outcome is even .

The next spin I stake £6 on odd .
The outcome is even .

The next spin I stake £15 on odd .
The outcome is even .

The next spin I stake £40 on odd .
The outcome is even .

The next spin I stake £90 on odd
The outcome is odd .
I win £180 .
Which gives me a profit of £25 .
Ill leave the table session .....
(approximately table time 8 minutes)

So we call it a day .....

Approximately table sessions time - 23 minutes .
Total profit overall - £57

Not bad for roughly 23 minutes work .
This is just a example but if you play live casino you will by now be able to see how this works .
The key is too walk away from that session on a high .
Some sessions you will have to pertcefere and may stake quite alot to drag very little profit from that session .
Remember there is roughly a 50/50 chance between even and odd .
Or black and red .
Regardless of there being a green zero the odds are still stacked in your favour .
If you play roulette on a regular basis at the casino or live casino from the comfort of your home .
Ask your self .
What is the most run of evens or odds have you seen during game play ???
Could you get a run of 20 evens on a table session .
I very much doubt it as you would have to be very unlucky to get that .
The point im making is on any table its only a matter of time before you win using these strategy .
But I would say it is ideal to have the funds to start with to back this method up in the first place .

To only deposit lets say £20 .
You are really taking it too chance to make that deposit
last if you get a run of bad spins .
But if you are studying the tables then you are minimising
your loss which gives you a better chance .

I hope reading this book as gave you the tools to make
your deposits more beneficial .
I will say that my methods will not work for everyone but
with responsible betting and knowledge then I cant see
why it will not work .
Patience is the key and to study the history of the tables to
give you the upper hand .
But everybody knows there is no no guarantees with
anything .
The remaining of the book I will give you key facts and tips
regarding roulette .

Top tip

Always stake on live tables online or at a casino as by doing this you know the wheels are not rigged and ultimately you are giving yourself a better chance of a return as ultimately its you choosing the outcome .

With a machine operated roulette wheel the outcome as already decided before you spin . Really it will not matter were you have placed your chip as if the machine does not want you to win they you not win .
Its as simple as that .

Im not saying you will not win but like the odds are more stacked against you .

Would you not want to give yourself the best possible chance ?

Study the table History

Always study the table sessions as this will give you the best possible outcomes before you stake .

As we have talked about during the book its common sense to back the opposite of a run of numbers as its mathematically in your favour .

It will give you a better possible outcome .

Live session table myth

Some would say That a roulette table live session with very few players that the odds are against you as the sessions will be focussed on the betting strategy that are being placed by the very few .
Basically slowing the ball down on a spin or trying to help the outcome .

With a Build up of players on a live session it is more or less impossible to keep track of the table covered giving you the advantage as strategy go unnoticed but like I say this is myth .

Can a dealer control were the ball lands ?

Its impossible for the dealer to anticipate where the ball will land .

casinos have strict rules and preventions in place to ensure that each spin of the wheel is fair and random .

Even if the dealer was the best in the world they would never be able to predict the exact number , colour it would land on .

Different versions available online live roulette

Notes

Profit

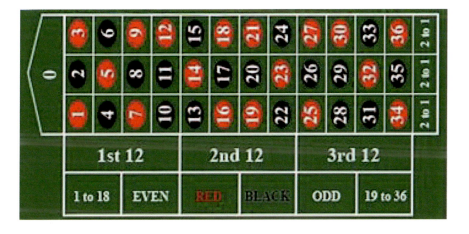

www.ingramcontent.com/pod-product-compliance
Lightning Source LLC
Chambersburg PA
CBRC091952080326
40690CB00053B/579